ST LUCY

1

2

4 3

5 6

ST PETER

ST ANDREW

7

8

ST JAMES

10 11

9

ST JOSEPH

26

12

13

14

15

16

ST THOMAS

ST JOHN

25

17

24

23

19

ST PHILIP

18

ST GEORGE

ST MICHAEL

21 22

CHRISTCHURCH

20

SPEIGHTSTOWN

HOLETOWN

BRIDGETOWN

OISTINS

1   Mount Gay Distillery   12   Welchman Hall Gully
2   St Nicholas Abbey   13   Harrison's Cave
3   Cherry Tree Hill   14   Villa Nova
4   Wildlife Reserve   15   St John's Church
5   Farley Hill
6   Morgan Lewis   Zoo Park
7   Chalky Mount

BARBADOS
Portrait of an Island

Dick Scoones

First published 1990

Published by MACMILLAN EDUCATION LTD
London and Basingstoke
Associated companies and representatives in Accra, Auckland, Delhi, Dublin, Gaborone, Hamburg, Harare, Hong Kong, Kuala Lumpur, Lagos, Manzini, Melbourne, Mexico City, Nairobi, New York, Singapore, Tokyo

ISBN 0 – 333 – 53432 – 8

Printed in Hong Kong

A CIP catalogue record for this book is available from the British Library.

Designed by Behram Kapadia

4

Introduction

It is a sad fact that many of the most colourful corners of the globe have been irreparably harmed by the tourism which their exotic charms have attracted. There are, however, beautiful and interesting places, Barbados being one of them, which have been exposed to the pressures imposed by tourism and have even encouraged tourism to dominate the economy, but have not been totally gobbled up.

Barbados has some of the finest beaches and most comfortable hotels in the world. It is also much more than its popular image might suggest. It is an island steeped in history, offering a wealth of interest to the visitor far beyond its exquisite rum punch and white sand. This is an island with its own character and sophistication, its own unique style.

On compiling this collection of photographs I have tried to present a view of the island as a visitor sees it. I have found in Barbados an island of great natural beauty and vibrance which is very different, both physically and culturally, from any others I have visited. But to compare the islands is a rather pointless exercise. There are horses for courses, and we each have our favourite for a multitude of reasons. Barbados is often criticised for being too 'developed and commercialised'. Certainly, a visitor does not suffer any of the deprivations common to countries of the Third World. Donkey carts and open-sided buses are something of the past. Nevertheless, Barbados is still a very young culture, the assimilation of many old cultures, which is growing and maturing. And it is a welcoming island; almost half a million visitors come here each year. Above all, Barbados is a perfect example of how a society which is in a stage of transition between being a traditional economy and an emerging industrial economy, and which has a pragmatic approach to economic progress, is able to develop tourism to its advantage.

Furthermore, it is with a feeling of relief that a visitor senses that Barbados is a society with its own dynamism and energy, and that if tourists should ever forsake the island for other destinations, Bajans would just change tack and go on living their own successful lives.

A Century of Tourism

From the arrival of the first British settlers in 1627 until quite recently Barbados was an island dependent on agriculture. At first it was tobacco, cotton and ginger. Then came sugar cane, based on technology brought from Brazil by Dutch immigrants in the seventeenth century, and it was on sugar that the island's prosperity was founded for the next three hundred years.

The development of tourism was by no means sudden. Since the end of the nineteenth century the hotels on the east coast, linked to Bridgetown by a regular train service, had been attracting tourists (mostly from Guyana and Trinidad) who visited the island on cruise ships. So when the sugar industry was

For My Parents

Acknowledgements

I would like to thank the many people who have
helped get *Barbados — Portrait of an Island* off the
ground, especially Sunniva Harte, without whose great
encouragement this book would still be a dream. The
late Ronald Tree, to whose published work I have
referred, and Colin Hudson, whose guidance has been
indispensable, also deserve special mention. Jill and
Jimmy Walker and their 'Best of Barbados' team have
been most generous with their assistance throughout
the project and Jill very kindly painted the maps
for me. To all the others who have helped in so
many ways and, of course, to those whose
images appear within these pages, I also extend
my sincere thanks.

in particular distress in the 1880s and 1930s, tourism was already able to make a significant contribution to the economy. But the final transfer from being a sugar island to being an island reliant in major part on hotel-based tourism was dramatic; in 1960 sugar still accounted for 90 per cent of the island's export revenue. However when the world sugar market plummeted in the 1980s, tourism was ready to fill the breach, and by 1988 sugar's share of the island's revenue had been reduced to a mere 30 per cent.

Around the Island

For an island just 21 miles long and 12 miles wide Barbados offers a staggering variety of coastline from wild, windswept beaches to placid, blue-water bays. The reason for such diversity lies in the geographical distribution of the islands of the Lesser Antilles which stand as a breakwater between the Atlantic Ocean and the Caribbean. The north and east shores of Barbados not only take the brunt of the heavy Atlantic seas but they also take the force of the prevailing easterly Trade Winds. And in the lee of the island, on the south and east coasts, the centres of population shelter. North Point, where the angry Atlantic waves have been thundering into the rugged cliffs for millions of years, presents one of the most unexpected but unforgettably awesome sights the island has to offer. Not far to the east, at Pie Corner, where the waves still thunder and the surf is high, young lads jump off the rocks and ride the waves on home-made surf boards.

It is a shame that when most visitors do their round-the-island tour they leave out St Lucy and the northern tip of the island. Instead, they take the road north to Speightstown and then veer east across the island to St Nicholas Abbey and the Wildlife Park. On past St Nicholas Abbey, this road leads up through a dark

tunnel of mahogany trees to the top of Cherry Tree Hill. It opens up quite suddenly into a spectacular panorama which takes in almost the entire length of the east coast, the parishes of St Andrew and St Joseph and the aptly-named Scotland district. The view of these green hills, only 1200 feet at their highest, is a wonderful surprise for the visitor who expects to find Barbados a flat island. In the far distance, rising out of the haze of Atlantic sea spray, is a small community which rejoices in the name of Bathsheba. In days gone by, when holiday resorts prided themselves on great walks, fresh air and marvellous views, Bathsheba was the pearl of the island, the choice for summer holidays and weekend picnics.

Alas, tastes changed. The railway track to Bridgetown has long since disappeared, Bathsheba is no longer a

machineel, mangrove and white cedar trees. Many of these trees have now gone but, viewed from the sea, the coastline still appears green and undeveloped. The hotels, modern shopping malls and private residences, many of Palladian style set in spacious gardens with wide beachfronts and expansive sea views, have been assimilated comfortably into the existing blend of old, shuttered residences and diminutive chattel houses, and the whole west coast ambience is still most agreeable.

The coastline changes quite radically once you turn the corner south of Bridgetown. This is suburbia. It was this part of the island which developed most rapidly for tourism. There is little of the west coast's indulgence in grandiose architecture here. It is more modest in all respects. Yet the attractive architectural styles are many and absorbing and retain a distinctly individual flavour. It is also here that the incredible blueness of the sea is at its most vivid. Once you pass Aquatic Gap the reef starts to bare its teeth, the breeze picks up, and by the time you pass Oistins and reach Silver Sands you are into the waves that windsurfers' dreams are made of. Further eastwards, into seemingly uncharted territory, a string of unspoilt, secluded bays, with names almost unheard of like Harrismith and Bottom Bay, bring you eventually to the east coast and the imposing tower of the Anglican parish church of St John. From its cliff-top perch its congregation savours a fine view – a ten mile bank of surf which takes the eye northwards from Bathsheba to Cattlewash and Cherry Tree Hill and further still to Pico Teneriffe.

resort, and the mantle of tourism has passed to the south and west coasts. Now this desolate, exposed, eastern shoreline is better-known for its threatening breakers, its intrepid surfers, its weather-beaten black-bellied sheep (which most visitors mistake for goats), its balconied beach houses, its breathtaking sunrises, its sea grape trees and its peeling paint. It is a far cry from the west coast which faces directly into the Caribbean. Despite the peace of its leaning coconut palms and gently lapping waves, the west coast has a different pace of life, reserved for the worship of fun and sun; *Jolly Roger* trips, the whole gamut of water sports, hair braiding, rotund ladies from Dominica selling palm-woven sun hats and brazen Rastas going about their business selling Taiwanese shell necklaces from attaché cases. But all this has been a relatively recent development. Less than 40 years ago the whole length of the west coast was thick with coconut, casuarina,

The Towering Cane

The 'island tour' should not be a 'once round and that's it' trip. The centre of the island also deserves exploring. Forged into the hills deep in the parish of St Thomas are great chasms where the island's limestone cap split aeons ago. The exquisite Harrison's Cave is part of this geographical formation. Almost the last remaining vestiges of how the island must have been when the first settlers arrived in the seventeenth century, dark, concealed, cavernous ravines, are Turners Hall, Jack-in-Box and Welchman Hall Gully. In Welchman Hall Gully, the most interesting and the one which has become a popular walk, giant bamboo, mahogany and bearded fig trees stretch upwards in search of light, scarlet ginger lilies grow and African green monkeys live. It was probably to the straggly, hanging tendrils of the bearded fig tree that the Portuguese referred when they named the island *Los Barbados*, the bearded ones. Not far away, in the parish of St Peter, at a crossroads surrounded by cane fields, stands another pointer to how things were in bygone centuries; a delightful signpost directing the way to Four Hill, Sailor Gully, The Whim, Indian Ground and Six Men, names full of the frontier spirit.

Sugar cane, though much reduced, still seems to carpet the island. An aerial tour of the island, preferably between the months of August and January when the cane is in its fullest splendour, provides a new perspective not only on the plantation system and the sheer extent of the cane, but also on the island's varied topography and its great contrast of shorelines. Cane cutting starts around the last week in January, weather permitting, and by July the land has been shorn as clean as a spring ewe to await the next annual cycle. The rejuvenated Cropover festival at the beginning of August celebrates the end of the harvest. It is the island's biggest 'jump up', growing in importance, size and extravagance of colour year by year. It is a great spectacle.

Sugar may no longer be king in Barbados, but it still dominates the island. A drive across country in an open (right hand drive) car, engulfed by the towering, blue-tinged cane, is an unforgettable experience. Every so often the solid wall of rustling cane breaks to reveal another fine plantation house set back from the road and surrounded by tall cabbage palms. Occasional strings of schoolgirls, all giggles, in cerise, lime green or blue gingham uniforms and complete in poppysocks and braided hair, saunter past, spots of bright colour in the rural landscape. Or your concentration may be broken by a pair of white egrets checking any morsels which the grazing cattle might disturb, or by a mongoose scooting across the road. Rural buses are infrequent, and the unpredictable condition of the narrow country roads does not encourage motorbike ownership. So walking is not shirked. At any rate it can bring communications between visitor and visited that much closer. To offer a ride to a lady full of the morning's joys and bound for church, or to a smiling agricultural worker returning home after a long day in the fields, is a gesture of mutual benefit which seems wholly natural in Barbados.

In casual chat with the poor whites you might occasionally meet in St Johns or in one of the more isolated rural areas, it becomes possible to appreciate another view of island life. For almost certainly you are talking to a so-called 'red leg' whose ancestors came out as indentured servants or deportees in the early days of colonisation. Even today a faint Irish brogue is often detectable. Originally the term 'red leg' was probably a reference to skin which, largely because of generations of in-breeding, had no tolerance of the sun. As 'red legs', 'ecky-beckies' or 'poor Johnnie Bakras' the members of the poor white community have always evoked pity from their fellow Bajans. Despite their pretensions to the maintenance of racial purity, inter-racial relationships have been the natural outcome of indentured whites and blacks living alongside each other in subjugation for so many generations, and these days mixed marriages in the poorer communities are not uncommon. Many poor whites still feel bitter that

Maristela, a Brazilian model on assignment in Barbados

they have been cheated by Britain. Nevertheless, whatever their past, dreams of returning to the country which they may believe is still theirs, it is now accepted that their last remaining link with their roots hangs only on living room walls, the portrait of the young Queen Elizabeth, looking out through billowing net curtains across the ocean which brought their hapless forebears to the island so many years ago.

To get out into the island at weekends is to see it at its best; to see how Bajans enjoy themselves, picnicking, playing beach cricket, body surfing, burning off their natural exuberance for hours on end in the sea. On Saturday evenings girls cluster together in tight groups or promenade arm in arm, dressed to kill in frilly Hispanic frocks and red patent shoes to match; and local lads look the part, cool in dark glasses and the latest styles. The Sunday morning church parade is no less grand; a bevy of women of all ages, demure in lace two-pieces and extravagantly-veiled hats, and young boys in smart haircuts, sharply-cut suits and elasticated bow ties. The churches, chapels and assembly halls of so many denominations – the Moravians, the Church of God, the Mormons and scores more – send out the message of the gospel through doors flung open wide, to the accompaniment of tamborines and congregations of clapping hands and truly joyous voices. And on Friday mornings it is the turn of the Moslems, the communities of Asian and Arab descent whose ancestors came originally to Guyana and Trinidad, to congregate for morning prayers at the mosques in Bridgetown.

Whatever one's religion there is always need for prayer when one is in the vicinity of high speed city buses, the Government buses, blue and bullish, which declare 'radios, peanuts and snowcones' forbidden cargo; and the private yellow minibuses which blast their complement of girls in yellow hair rollers with the latest taste in reggae. They drive with quite alarming aggression along the roads which often lack both width and pavements. Thankfully, the trip around the island does not have to be at the behest of some break-neck bus driver. Hire a car for a few days and take the island in your own time. But bear in mind that leisure is taken very seriously here and some disregard for the stopwatch demands of the modern world is a prerequisite for anyone wishing to glean the maximum benefit from actually being in Barbados.

The Colonial Legacy

Largely because Barbados is 100 miles to the east of the other Leeward Islands and because reaching it by sail means having to beat laboriously against the wind, Barbados remained the exclusive colonial possession of Britain from 1627 until 1966, one of the few Caribbean territories not to change hands during its colonial history. The islanders even christened themselves 'Bimshire' as some suggestion that Barbados was just another British county. The British influence may now have ended, but the unmistakable stamp of the old mother country is still in evidence everywhere you turn. Communities such as Dover, Hastings and Worthing are located, as one might expect, on the south coast. In the country there are the villages of Cheltenham, Malvern, Harrow, Henley, Oxford and Cambridge, and plantations and Great Houses with names such as Bloomsbury, Newcastle, Bentleys and Clifton Hall. In the centre of Bridgetown there is Cheapside Market, Trafalgar Square and Nelson's statue, and narrow streets with names like Victoria Street, Coleridge Street and Swan Street which, true to traditional British town planning, worm their way through the capital.

Driving through the island, it becomes immediately obvious that Barbados is divided into the British system of community administration, parishes, each of the eleven parishes having its own imposing Anglican church. And such is the greenness of the fields and the frequency of tended front gardens that one can only be reminded of the English. The Andromeda Gardens on the east coast are a fine continuation of the horticultural heritage. A little further down the road the Atlantis and Kingsley Club Hotels positively wallow in the excellence of their traditional Sunday lunch. Just as celebrated, but on the west coast, is the afternoon tea served at the superb Coral Reef Club, a standard bearer in the tradition of fine Barbados hotels. It provides its guests with white rattan furniture, open terraces, shady casuarina trees, a magnificent view, luxuriant tropical gardens, an abundance of space and peace, all the ingredients necessary for anyone wishing to abandon the ghastly happenings of the real world. And for those guests who cannot live without the cricket scores, ghastly or not, there is the *Daily Telegraph* flown in from London.

Although it is fair to say that other sports, like Saturday horse racing or Sunday afternoon polo, are also well supported and help to preserve the Britishness of Barbados, it is cricket, whether it be at the Kensington Oval or on the beach, which is still the beloved national sport. It was cricket, of course, which sired the island's greatest heroes. The most acclaimed West Indian cricketer of all time, Gary Sobers, was knighted by the Queen in 1975 in a ceremony at the historic Garrison Savannah. But from Worrell, Walcott and Weeks, to Griffith, Hall, Marshall, Greenidge, Haynes and Garner, generations of Bajans became far more than simply local heroes; these are names which, in their time, have been almost as familiar in countries as distant as India, Australia and England as in their native land.

The Parliament Buildings, situated alongside the Careenage, dominate the centre of Bridgetown.

Established in 1639, the Barbados Parliament is actually the third oldest in the British Commonwealth. It still works along traditional Westminster lines and retains much of its original atmosphere. The fine Gothic chamber of the House of Assembly is overlooked by the monarchs of England set in stained-glass windows. They even include the victorious Roundhead, Oliver Cromwell, for whom Barbados held very little affection. Outside the Parliament Buildings stand guard unarmed, white-helmeted policemen of the Royal Barbados Police Force whose own continuation of the colonial tradition provides the island with the spectacle of mounted policemen and an excellent brass band.

As each year passes, however, the links with the colonial past weaken. Nowadays the USA and Canada, the country's foremost trading partners and major source of tourists, continue to exert an ever stronger influence on the island. Tourism, trade, television, investment, fast-food chains, property ownership, radio evangelism, music, educational opportunities, language and inter-government aid have all had their impact. Even the island's institutions are being induced to change. Prior to 1987 barristers-at-law may have been seen in the law courts, enrobed and bewigged, but now the wigs have gone and lawyers are called attorneys. And if proof were needed of where the islands of the East Caribbean feel their military protection lies, one only has to recall that in 1983 it was the United States who responded to the request by a number of East Caribbean nations to intervene in neighbouring Grenada after the bloody coup. The American staging post was Barbados. Despite the Americanisation of the island, however, there is an enduring Britishness in Barbados – the way the people are, the way the island is. Of course, things will change, although it would be pleasing to think that the historical heritage will be sustained and the atmosphere of the island as it now is will not die completely. If nothing else, there is always the Barbados telephone book to reassure you of the British connection. Its pages are full of Cumberbatches and Devonishes and names of the gentry of England, names given to the slaves on arrival in Barbados. This very day, in fact, I have met a black Bajan by the most unlikely name of Lochinvar MacDonald.

The Pride of Barbados

Probably the least obvious of the island's colonial legacies, yet arguably the most impressive are the Great Houses such as Sunbury, St Nicholas Abbey, Villa Nova and many others scattered across the island, the power house of the national economy in the age when sugar was king. Many plantations still have the derelict, vine-covered shells of the old wind-driven sugar mills and their old bell towers which were used for regulating the slaves' working day and for warning of impending hurricanes. Many of the 500 or so windmills that graced the landscape a century ago still remain. Only one, however, the Morgan Lewis mill which is preserved by the Barbados National Trust, still has its machinery intact. By the end of the seventeenth century the sugar boom was over. Increasing competition from other countries which went into sugar production resulted in a dramatic decline in the profitability of sugar for Barbados which hitherto had a virtual monopoly on the sugar trade. Hurricanes, the rapid exhaustion of the soil and the detrimental effects of absentee landlords added to the malaise in the industry. Some landowners made their fortunes and returned to England while others, less fortunate, lost everything to their creditors. Small holdings were absorbed into plantations, and as plantations grew in size so they decreased in number. The result of so much land changing hands was that, of the Great Houses, only Drax Hall, the island's oldest building, is still owned by the descendants of its original occupants.

Most of these properties and a number of other fine houses are opened to the public annually between January and March in an 'Open House' programme organised by the Barbados National Trust. The Trust has done much to preserve the island's heritage and to propagate a consciousness at all levels of Bajan society that what Barbados has in its historical, social and natural environment is very special. As much as anything else it is the architecture, a labyrinth of individual design, great and small, combining North European and Latin American influences, which distinguishes Barbados. Nevertheless, whilst the island would not wish to compete with Bermuda for prizes in perfection, there are many Bajans who are concerned that so many once-delightful residences, private and state-owned, now seem to be neglected or abandoned. Included amongst those buildings under threat, from progress rather than neglect, are the tiny pastel-coloured, wooden *chattel houses with their pocket-handkerchief gardens, shuttered windows, jalousies and airy porches. They are all over the island, overhung by the fleshy leaves of the ubiquitous breadfruit tree. The smallness of the chattel house has inevitably led to the modern vogue for owning a property with 'walls' and, although it is still such an essential part of the Barbados landscape, there is little doubt that the endearing chattel house will soon be no more than a relic of history.

No one could deny that Bajans have a great deal of self respect. They are proud of what they are, what they have and how they look, their past and

*The name *chattel house* is derived from the days of the plantation system when a plantation labourer was expected to be able to move from one plantation to the next. His house was part of his *chattel*, so it had to be constructed in such a way that it could be easily dismantled and transported.

Alberta Collymore, outside her home in Boscobelle, St Peter

their present, both nationally and personally. The environment may not yet be of interest to all Bajans, but there appears to be a healthy awareness. On the beaches, municipal workers ensure that Barbados has some of the whitest and cleanest beaches in the world. In the city there is a preference not for gratuitous urban graffiti but for colourful murals depicting national, social and Rastafarian themes. And in the country increasing energy is being devoted to worthwhile projects, one of the most recently completed being the unique walk-through Wildlife Reserve in St Peter. Created in three acres of mahogany trees, the Wildlife Reserve is now a centre for the breeding and study of African green monkeys which were imported from West Africa in the seventeenth century and now live wild in the island. It is wonderfully refreshing to walk around the reserve and enjoy the atmosphere of freedom, not imprisonment, which has resulted from thoughtful design and a concern for the habitat of the animals. It is the drive and imagination of people like Canadian Jean Baulu, the reserve's founder-director, which have been instrumental in making the island what it is. Bajans do not forget this. Moreover, the many people whose enthusiasm and commitment to Barbados have put the island on the map are not distanced from the community by TV studios or security fences; the island is not big enough for that. Whether they are statesmen, cricketers, artists or calypsonians, they are still very much a part of the community. Barbados remembers its past achievers; Samuel Jackman Prescod, the first non-white to become a Member of Parliament; Conrad Reeves, the island's first Chief Justice and the first black Bajan to be knighted; Dr Charles Duncan O'Neal, the radical mulatto politician; his successor and the first premier of Barbados and of the aborted West Indies Federation of 1958, the progressive Sir Grantley Adams; the nation's first prime minister, Errol Barrow, and his successor, Tom Adams.

And it is not necessary to be a politician to be appreciated. Nailed to the roots of an ancient tree in the depths of Welchman Hall Gully is a small, rudimentary plaque. It simply states: 'Remember Ronald Tree'. In addition to the foundation of the Barbados National Trust, Tree's many contributions to the life of the island included the creation of two of its best known landmarks: the majestic Heron Bay and Sandy Lane Hotels. This most informal yet poignant memorial to one of the many immigrants who have contributed so much to the island over the years stands with flying fish, rum punch and the chicken gizzards of Granny's Restaurant in Oistins as one of my first and fondest memories of the island.

The First Bajans

Christopher Columbus came to the Caribbean four times, but it is assumed that either he never saw Barbados or he simply decided not to stop here. Instead, it was later Portuguese *conquistadores* who were the first to land on the island in 1536. It is thought probable that the island lacked the economic potential of other neighbouring islands and it was left to the British to claim it for King James I in 1625. The first shipload of settlers arrived two years later, in February 1627, landing on the west coast at Holetown. The first Bajans were mainly young Englishmen from the West Country, middle class with royalist sympathies, for whom the uncertain prospects of the New World seemed a very much more attractive option than remaining in a country racked by poverty and, 25 years later, by civil war. Depending on their means, they could either buy or lease smallholdings or estates on the island. For many others who took the westward passage the circumstances were rather more compelling. Twelve thousand recalcitrant Irishmen were deported to the West Indies in 1649 by Oliver Cromwell when he brought Ireland to heel. It is said that to have someone 'Barbadosed' even became a generic term. Thousands more, royalists captured at the Battle of Worcester, were deported in 1652, and many of those who escaped the gallows of Judge Jeffries' 'Bloody Assizes' following the Monmouth Rebellion in 1685 met a similar fate. And last but by no means least there were the poor, landless labourers enlisted as indentured servants in a desperate attempt to escape the dire straits they faced in Britain. For a fixed term of forced labour they could purchase the promise of freedom and a smallholding. Unfortunately for these white slaves, the fact that their servitude was only short term, say ten years, meant that their masters had no long term interest in them and, as a result, they often received treatment considerably worse than their black counterparts.

These, however, were not the first occupants of Barbados. From about 400 to 600 AD the island was occupied by Salanoid-Barrancoid Amerindians. They were replaced by the Arawaks 200 years later, and their 400 year occupancy of Barbados ended in 1200 AD when they were driven north and off the island by the cannibalistic Carib Indians. Why the Caribs then left the island is not known, but by the time the British arrived in 1627 it is probable that no Indians had lived on the island for 100 years or so. It is known, however, that the first settlers brought some Arawaks from South America, probably from nearby Guyana, to advise on the best way to exploit the land for agriculture. The fruits and vegetables eaten in Barbados today including cassava, yams, limes, pineapples, melons, were all introduced by these Arawaks.

Development of the island was rapid. Only 25 years after the first settlers were building themselves crude dwellings of wood and palm thatch, the island's first Great Houses had been built.

The dense forest which had originally covered the island was quickly levelled and replaced by sugar cane, a crop whose harvest and profitability was only made viable by the availability of a massive pool of black slave labour. Indeed, the very first settlers to arrive in Holetown had brought with them a number of black slaves who had probably been taken off a slave galleon encountered on passage. Additional labour to work the new sugar plantations was to be procured from predominantly Dutch and Portuguese slave galleons which were already doing a brisk trade in African slaves with the Spanish colonies in the Caribbean. It was sugar and the plantation system, therefore, which were to graft the culture of Britain, the world's most advanced nation at the time, and the primitive cultures of West Africa, and together they would sculpt the progressive nation we see today.

Slavery

The island's development was by no means plain sailing; there were highs and lows, both politically and economically. Serious communal conflict was reported as early as 1628 when the two rival colonial settlements of Holetown and Bridgetown fought each other and the issue of allegiance to the crown during the years of the Civil War in England was always a source of social strife. In 1651 Cromwell's fleet even attacked the royalist island and succeeded in expelling the Governor, Lord Willoughby. When times were good in Barbados, when society had stabilised and sugar was king, the dynastic slave-owning plantocracy must have lived a life of enviable luxury. But nowhere in the British Empire could life have seemed more precariously balanced. There were frequent epidemics of one kind or another; smallpox, dysentry and yellow fever had a habit of decimating the population, with no discrimination between black and white, rich or poor, and anyone living into his 40s had far surpassed the average life expectancy. Simply making ends meet must have been a problem for a large percentage of the island's inhabitants. The honeymoon for sugar production was well and truly over by the beginning of the eighteenth century, and matters were made worse by the determination of the British Government to impose oppressive taxes and trade embargoes on sugar. In the mid-seventeenth century things had looked good in Barbados and the population reached 50,000. By the turn of the century the population had been halved.

To add to these problems there was always the fear of slave uprisings. By 1667 there were over 40,000 slaves and at the peak of the plantation system slaves outnumbered free whites by 4:1. The Establishment therefore had to live on its wits, controlling the island with vigilance and severely restricting the movements and association of the potentially volatile slave population. Native languages and music as well as Christian worship were seen as a threat by slave owners. This suppression of African culture was made easier for the planters by the fact that the slaves had all been taken from different regions of West Africa. There was therefore no common tribe or language to bind the slaves together. The planters were also helped by the existence of a buffer class of free blacks and mulattoes. The blacks had usually won their freedom through infirmity or as a result of the benevolence of a minority of compassionate individual planters. The mulattoes were either the progeny of illicit liaisons between a planter and his slaves or were creole slaves imported from other islands. With only a few notable exceptions this mulatto class was happy to accept the privileges which accrued from the system, and they assisted in its perpetuation. Blacks also found that, in time, they too could improve their lot better by working within the system, and 'trusty' slaves became an important factor in the ability of the Establishment to keep the system going. By the 1750s the slave population in Barbados had stabilised. Figures which show the slave trade reaching its peak between 1776 – 90 conceal the fact that Barbados had become the centre for a very active re-export trade in slaves in the region.

The first attempts to outlaw slavery were made in 1655 by the Quakers. Their protests were not enthusiastically received in the West Indies. On the contrary, the slave-owning plantocracy closed ranks in their determination to maintain the system. Liberals and abolitionists in America and England urged that the slaves be free to worship, but the Church held that blacks had no soul and therefore could not be Christians. More importantly, the Bajan Establishment realised that Christianity taught that man is equal, regardless of colour. Any concession to slavery in Barbados, therefore, would not only have been incompatible with the perpetuation of the privileged lifestyle of the white plantocracy, it would also have provided moral grounds for the abolition of slavery, on which the profitability of sugar cane was dependent. Whilst the Anglican Church on the island stood firm behind the slave owners, the Protestant Evangelist movement continued to denounce slavery and today the legacy of the Evangelists' crusade is clear to see. They opened the door for Protestant free churches, especially from America, and the island is now abuzz with the worship of over 120 individual Protestant denominations. The British Parliament eventually abolished slavery in 1807, although it was not until 1834 that the Barbados Parliament agreed to pass its own Abolition of Slavery Bill. Until then slaves continued to be traded at auction. As Ronald Tree relates in his comprehensive *History of Barbados*, even George Washington took advantage of the auctions in Barbados (the only country he visited outside America). It was to here that he once sent a male slave whom he found difficult to manage.

Even after the Abolition of Slavery slaves were not free. A system of 'apprenticeship' was instituted, ensuring that slaves would be held in bondage for a further four years. Emancipation proper only came in 1838, although what that has meant, in terms of economic self-determination in the years since, has been a continuing source of debate.

In spite of generations of subjugation, the resilient African spirit and identity has survived, and the grass-roots Barbados of today still bears traces of the African influence in its music, food, herbal medicines and, in particular, its language, a Bajan creole which is virtually unintelligible to non-Bajans. Although it contains very few words which are directly descended from African languages Bajan creole bears a marked similarity to the creole spoken in West Africa today. In the years following Emancipation the cultural awareness of the black community throughout the West Indies gained momentum, culminating in the 1920s and 1930s in the 'Back to Africa' movement of Jamaican Marcus Garvey. More recently the Caribbean has felt the influence of the Rastafarian cult which, like Garvey, also preaches that one day all Afro-Caribbeans will return to Africa. But probably the most apparent example of the way the plantation system has etched itself on modern Barbados society is found in the structure of the Bajan family. Slaves were not generally encouraged to form stable relationships or create family units. It is hardly surprising, therefore, that today, albeit in an island in which Christianity is alive and well, the Christian convention of marriage and monogamy is not strictly adhered to. Throughout the Caribbean some 70 per cent of all births, often of uncertain paternity, take place out of wedlock, and it is not uncommon for a woman to have had children by several different partners.

The Image

There can be few parts of the world which bask in as many preconceptions as the West Indies. For years we have been led to believe in this tropical paradise of endless sun, endless carnival, smiling faces, steel bands, exotic fruits, billowing sails, piña coladas and crystal clear water.

Such an image is not entirely the fanciful creation of some advertising agency, although the reality is perhaps somewhat less romantic. The particular island, the season, and one's accommodation have much to do with the impression created. Nevertheless, life in the islands does have a warmth, a timelessness, which makes the whole Caribbean experience very special. Barbados itself has one of the world's most perfect tropical climates with an average of about eight hours of sunshine a day all year round. Daytime temperatures hover between 26°C and 30°C, and nights are pleasantly cool for most of the year. The months from February to June are normally dry, but as the humidity increases in July the weather becomes more fickle, ranging from the sublime to the ridiculous. On the days of the sublime it is hard to imagine the days of the ridiculous. Barbados is on the periphery of the hurricane belt and has only been hit by four really serious blows since the British arrived in 1627, the last being in 1955. During 'hurricane season', the months from June to October, tropical storms are quite frequent, and it is these storms, starting as depressions in mid-Atlantic, which develop into hurricanes, winds of up to 200 mph which rip through the Caribbean with tedious regularity, leaving great swathes of destruction in their wake. As the Bajans say 'June too soon, July standby, August a must, September remember, October all over'. This is not strictly true. I write in mid-September and of the eight tropical storm warnings issued since July, the only one which has developed into a full-scale hurricane has been Hugo which mercifully missed Barbados but went on to devastate Montserrat and leave a trail of appalling destruction which stretched from the Leeward Islands as far as the Carolinas. Seasonal rains usually start in July and have reached their peak by November.

However, the rain rarely persists and overcast days are infrequent. Nevertheless, when the rains do start they are welcomed by the islanders, bringing relief to the vegetation, beleaguered after months of drought. But drought or not, this is an island of extraordinary colour. The pervasive greenness is laced with frequent celebrations of brilliance – reds, yellows, and blues – which add spice to every day; a fleeting glimpse of the sea, azure and green; long stretches of the whitest sand; yellow-breasted bananaquits; the occasional emerald-plumed humming bird darting along the hibiscus border; green-backed lizards; waxy, scarlet ginger lilies; orange and red-striped 'Sunshine' bread shops; roadside fruit stalls; the 'Snow on the Mountain' which blooms at Christmas alongside the dramatic crimson of the poinsettia; the pinks and creams of the heavenly frangipani; the flamboyant tree whose flaming red blossom lasts throughout the summer months; the brilliant yellow bignonia, or 'Shower of Gold', which covers the old windmills in April; and the banks of bougainvillea and the 'Pride of Barbados', the island's national flower.

Visitors to the Caribbean often complain about the high prices. Things certainly are not cheap in Barbados and one can only say that, with the all too frequent exception of car rental, at least the consumer gets good quality in return for the margin of difference in prices. Unlike its neighbours St Lucia, Grenada, St Vincent and Dominica, all particularly fecund volcanic islands, Barbados is a coral island. Although some of the parishes, such as St Thomas, might appear to be lush and fertile, the island's climatic extremes of rain, drought and temperature and its limestone cap mean that the soil is not easily cultivated. The success of sugar as a cash crop was due to the ready availability of slave labour and to the small population which did not demand a vast acreage to meet its own needs. Most of the island's arable land could therefore be rotated with sugar. Although sugar cane still covers 30 per cent of the total area of the island and sugar has emerged, once again, from the doldrums, landowners are now faced with some radical decisions as to how they should use their property in the future; for the greater production of dairy products and livestock, a diversification in crops, the development of Barbados into a golfers' paradise, the expansion of industrial plant. There are a number of ways the island could go.

For many Bajans life is not always easy. The obvious style and enjoyment of life and the importance attached to the more visible consumer items such as cars and videos perhaps conceal a standard of living which is still a monthly calculation. The unemployed do find some relief, perhaps, in social security benefits. Nevertheless, 22 per cent of the work force is currently without work, either by choice or through lack of jobs. This is not to suggest that visitors may expect to find a depressed economy. On the contrary, the immediate impression is one of general well-being, a busy island with its own vitality and atmosphere.

One does not have to scratch too far below the

and there are constant reminders that Bajans of all colours can break down the social barriers and pull together whenever they choose. As they say 'All o' we is one'.

Tropical Magic

Social stability in Barbados is a direct reflection of the efforts of the Government to serve the people. Things work here; public utilities, telephones, public transport, socialised medicine, roads. Heavy-handed police, petty bureaucratic corruption, political excess and extremes of economic disparity, which are the curse of many developing nations, are happily not a part of Bajan life. Instead, the law is seen to be fair, churches are well patronised, and education and equal opportunity are for everyone. The combination of so many positive features creates a peacefulness which is the perfect backdrop for a holiday.

The moment you step off the plane you feel you are under a delightful tropical assault, the smells, the noise, the banana trees. Some equatorial countries smell of sandalwood or coffee, or cloves perhaps. Duty free emporia, the destiny of more and more islands, smell of electronic hardware and styrene wrapping. Barbados, for me at least, smells of the sea, rum and West Indian cooking. But although the food in the island's top hotels and restaurants is excellent, there is a shortage of more modest eating places which offer Bajan specialities. Beyond 'peas and rice', flying fish, king fish, another fish misleadingly called dolphin, and West Indian vegetables such as squash, pumpkin, cristophene, okra and aubergine, it is probable that there will not be much on a Bajan menu to satisfy the gastronome in search of strictly local cuisine. The Bajan home offers little greater variety. Two dishes which are descended directly from the days of slavery are cou-cou, a corn meal pudding, and salt fish.

surface of Bajan society to realise that this is a complex nation which is still shaking off the shackles of a deep-seated inferiority inherited from the colonial era. It is hardly surprising. After all, until relatively recently the black and white communities were locked in a permanent state of antagonism, if not confrontation. Discrimination did not end with the abolition of slavery. There are people in Barbados today who took part in the riots of 1937 at a time when 70 per cent of the population still did not have the vote, and there are people whose grandparents were probably involved in the riots of 1876 which led to the death or execution of 390 Bajans (the modern day equivalent of approximately 160,000 deaths in a riot in Britain).

However, for the vast majority of Bajans, independence from Britain in 1966 brought a spirit of national pride which nurtures reconciliation and not confrontation. Even though this has not meant racial integration – mixed marriages are still rare – Barbados impresses the visitor with its tolerant, multi-racial coexistence,

A favourite Bajan snack is a fish cutter, a fish steak served in a hamburger roll, or an Indian-inspired, curry-flavoured roti, a rolled chapati of chicken or meat and potato. Whilst the standard Bajan menu might be lacking in imagination, the Bajan bar is certainly not. There are some lively sundowners; Carnival Jump Up, Pink Cricketer, Between the Sheets, Desperate Virgin, Hurricane, Pirate's Revenge and Shark's Tooth to name but a few. Rum, of course, is in plentiful supply, and it is all around you in some form or other, be it in the trucks of molasses which dawdle along the country roads, barrels of rum punch on the *Jolly Roger*, or the myriad of little bars known as 'rum shops'.

At the end of another Barbados day savour the moments of tropical magic; the nights of steel bands, reggae and calypso, fireflies, limbo dancing, the cacophony of crickets and tree frogs. They are not easily forgotten. And when you think it is time for bed go via Baxters Road, for this is where Bajans traditionally gravitate to round off their night when all else is closed. Here the hum of the rum shops and billiard halls, the slurping of Banks beer, the crashing of dominoes on wood and the hissing of great slabs of king fish frying in massive woks only ends under protest at dawn.

TO DREAM

of the sounds of life as tropical songs
of breaking waves
of silence buried in Carib caves
of cricket and crickets and tiny tree frogs
they fill each night
as vivid colours fill each day
all blues and greens and in betweens
whitest Cattlewash surf
cerise bougainvillea
pearls of sweat on ebony hides
Ambre Solaire for skin that's fair
scanty lime green bikinis
to rattle the imagination
and shimmer the fronds of leaning coconut palms
even scanter thoughts of murky Manhatten mists

lotus eaters not caring less
no loti
just eating and sunning and swimming and sipping
lying floating kicking fantasising ecstasising
timeless smiles
and endless time to stare
into the vast nothingness of tropical days and
                                    yawning skies
at the sheer gall of red starfish
the absurdity of mustard-plumed coral
and cruising amphibians
with eyes in their tails and rainbow pretensions
ugly crabs laughing sideways
as self-conscious as the empty green coconut shell
lurking half-buried in the sand
abandoned

alone to tell whose hand held it in life
whose lips sucked out its young existence
what tree in what parish on what island
nurtured it to this end

a fleeting celebration of yellow
enter windsurfer, left,
on the warming Trade Winds
jibing and planing over the dry blueness
leaping the reef
enjoying the moment she knows is hers
enter cheeky bananaquit, right,
on another raid of sweetness and sugar
enter blissful thoughts, centre,
day return castaways
no videos no radios
no beachboy romeos
'Thank God' I hear them say
this is the life wish you were here
flying fish sandwiches stacks of cold beer
soporific tones of a day dissolving
happy hour and shadows lengthening
no need for clocks
rum and soda time
hungry clouds waiting furtively under the horizon
to guzzle up the sun and snuff out
a thousand moments of anticipation
thoughts of paradise
bounding across the closing window of the day
once more
suspended in this playground of superlatives

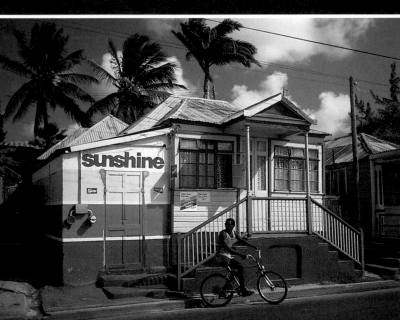

Illustrations

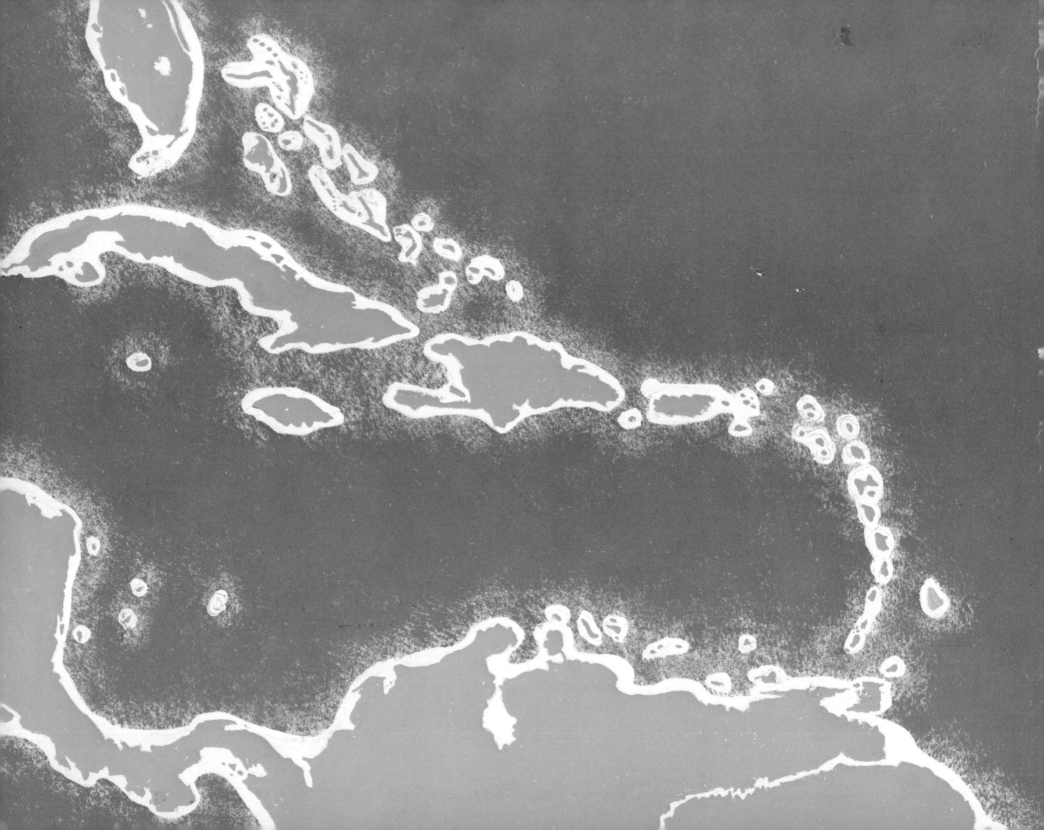